Delicious

PADRAIG REGAN

THE LIFEBOAT
POETRY PAMPHLET #1

First published in 2016
by The Lifeboat
www.lifeboatbelfast.co.uk

Printed in Belfast
by Cathedral Graphics

A CIP record for this book
is available from the British Library

ISBN 978-0993584107

2 4 6 8 10 9 7 5 3 1

CONTENTS

10 Game Fowls

after Juan Sánchez Cotán's 'Still Life with Game Fowl, Vegetables and Fruits'

Five of the six sparrows tied
to a pole have turned their
heads to where a bundle of
orange carrots bruised with
purple, or purple carrots
blushing, underline a few
inches of black space &
describe a trajectory to the
base of a white cardoon
whose architectural sweep
curves towards a pair of
partridges displaying the
tincture of their azure chests
& putting to shame a pair of
finches which intersect
between the partridges &
the apples suspended on
individual strings which
twist together like a maypole
adjacent to where the black
background snags on a twig
with three radiant lemons &

all this above the plinth
where Juan Sánchez Cotán
has faux-engraved his
signature & added the date
1602: one year before he
gave up eating the flesh of
beasts & fowls & joined the
Order of Carthusians in
Granada.

Aubade with Half a Lemon on the Summer Solstice

Sleep was a paltry wafer
after we'd come back
from watching the tide
expose the beach's softer
districts & the sun
beginning to spill through
a murder-hole in an
architrave of clouds. The
open half of a lemon had
been left in the kitchen,
weeping into the grain of
the table. The table
corresponds with the
woody pips; the lemon
corresponds with a
breakfast of fried eggs &
butter melting into a slice
of toast. It donated its
other half to the piquancy
of gin & tonics. I squeeze
out what's left of the juice
& a paper cut I didn't
know I had begins to sing
Puccini's Vissi d'Arte.

Poem on the First Warm Day of the Year

The carrots might yet
find themselves in a
soup incandescent with
chilli flakes & cumin
seeds, but then again
maybe we'll leave them
to their cellophane
bivouac in the fridge
& go out late in the
morning for coffee or
milkshakes & maybe the
willows in the Botanic
Gardens with their
branches shimmying
like a good, thick wig
will invite us to sit on
the grass & we couldn't
possibly refuse, but by
then our faces will be
exactly like the carrots
as they give themselves
up to the butter & the
heat, so we'll cross
the river in search of
ice-cream, then walk
around the park until
our legs resent us, &
to reward their patient
service we'll stop on a
bench & smoke & one

of us will remind the
other about the pub
on the route home but
when – finally! – we
find a seat on the terrace
we'll decide that all we
want is a glass of Coke
& the froth will taste
like the beard of God.

Vanity with Cantaloupe

By then the melon was more
like a half-deflated football; the
rind was more like leather than
anything you would call a skin.

It surrendered all too easily to
the dint of the fingers, was all
too willing to open itself in
response to the paring knife —

I should have guessed its secrets
then. But I pressed on, down
through the boneless, coral-
coloured flesh &

let it fall, bisected, on the
counter-top in a slick of its own
escaped juices. It confirmed
what I knew all along:

that the seeds would be pouched
in a lace of fungus, that the
centre of the fruit would tend
towards deliquescence.

There was nothing to be done
but swaddle it in plastic bags &
dump it in the trash like two
halves of a split millstone,

but something about its downy,
grey lanugo of mould, its fragile
self-composure, brought to
mind the bodies

of old men with their skins
loose & thin as jellyfishes' &
barely able to hide the plum-red
lattices of capillaries.

Love Poem with Sandwiches

I had this plan: to come up
with titles for poems like
*Nocturne with a Bottle of
Sparkling Wine* or *Aubade
with Figs & Water Glass* but
instead of writing the poems
I'd just copy the titles onto
slices of white bread using
blue ink & a brush & then
I'd use them to make
sandwiches with things like
tamarind & Roquefort &
whole thickets of herbs to
mask the rusty taste of the
ink & feed them to this guy I
was dating because the first
time I saw him naked in
daylight the hairs on his
belly reminded me of that
texture you find at the centre
of a loaf when you grip the
crusts & pull it apart.

Epithalamium with Peach Melba

The account omits any mention
of music, but when I picture the
scene — the Duc d'Orléans at
the head of the table

& the famously talented young
singer beside him & a swan
sculpted in ice with the space
between its scapulars

mounded with ice-cream &
peaches — all I hear is *Duftender
Raum, zur Liebe geschmückt,
nehm' euch nun auf.*

Any passable attempt at the dish
requires one peach per person,
cut in half & poached with an
irresponsible amount of sugar.

Serve it on the patio, in cut-
glass 20s bowls so your guests
can marvel at the contrast
between the orange peaches

& the deep cerise of the
raspberry sauce. Light candles
to keep the wasps away. If
nothing else it sure feels great

to slip your thumb under a
peach stone & push it out. & if
it tears & a little sticky juice
spurts from it,

remember that it is only a
prelude to the moment you bite
in. Remember that eating is
always an act of theft.

Aoshima

I imagine you stopping
somewhere along the
infinite ribbon of white
sand & kneeling down to
give your dog one last
scratch behind the ear,
then taking off & burying
your shoes. You wade into
the water which is
decorated by the sun with
a thousand scraps of
lemon rind & warmer
than you expected. If you
can, stay true to west by
south west until once
again you feel the
feathering of kelp
between your toes, climb
out onto a new beach,
walk to a low brick wall
which marks the
boundary where grass
rubs against sand, & sit &
wait until the island's
hundred cats introduce
themselves, individually,
to your ankles.

Red Interior with Savoy Cabbage

The white ceiling bounces off
the crimson walls; one wall
vibrates with yellow light from
the window; the window
reduces the street to a framed
geometry; the geometry of the
street, the window, the walls
cannot account for the curvy
bulk of the brown leather sofa;
the sofa is set off with white
cushions; the cushions are
fringed with gold tassels; the
colours of the sofa, cushions &
tassels are reconfigured in the
rosewood escritoire with its
brass drawer-handles & fantails
of papers; the papers spill over
onto the floor & cut an
awkward tessellation on the red
carpet; at the centre of the
carpet something green is made
greener by its opposition to the
red shag: a savoy, cut perfectly
through its middle & lying
docile as though listening to
voices from the room above,
grunts & mutterings, the sound
of someone flicking a switch.

An Exhibit Illustrating the Life of Neolithic Man

It was a lie when I said
the birds were fake & I
knew it was a lie. I'm
terribly sorry. I offered
to show you around the
museum   expecting
easy talk about post-
war abstraction, the St
Ives School. We were
presented   with   a
diorama of axe-heads,
wolf-skins,   our   small
reflections in the birds'
large eyes. Your horror
sunk   into   the   gallery
like snow. I'm tasting
it still when I can't
distract myself from all
the stains of all the lies
I've ever told & that
I've   listened   to,
knowing that they were
lies but desperate to
accept them. & the
next   time   we   talk
they'll be there, taking
the shape of a ceramic
bird which neither of
us will recognise.

Centrefold

after Tomás Hiepes' 'Still Life with Birds & Hare'

There is a symmetry in
this: it all pivots
around that plucked
bird who shows not
just its flushed &
pimpled skin but, in a
bowl below its feet, its
own red entrails. From
there, other hanging
things fan out. So a
pair of partridges are
balanced by another
pair of partridges; a
duck with all its
feathers is offset by a
hare; & crammed in at
either edge, a pigeon &
a naked duck complete

the overall effect
which is like a sort of
tattered curtain,
making the table a sort
of stage, on which a
drama of meat & eggs
& giblets is playing
itself out. The knife in
left corner is integral.

Vanity with Eggs & Giblets

What cruel joke is this?
The similarity of shape
between the eggs & the
small kidneys seems to
be making some kind
of point, which is not,
as you might expect,
negated but
compounded by the
differences of colour &
texture. The glistening
innards by themselves
would unfold much the
same story, but all too
directly; it is their
pessimistic answer to
the eggs' question
which you'll remember
in a few years from
now when you decide
it's time to take the
curtains off the mirrors
& see again your eyes
with your own eyes, &
in the second which
intersects between your
foot slipping from the
rung & the floor
meeting you abruptly,
you'll be thinking of
the large & hilarious
absurdity of this lunch.

Aubade with Seagulls Eating a Cottage Loaf

Think of it as something
made, something worked—
over; as evidence that
someone you have never met

has a certain knack of teasing
out & folding back the dough
that is unique to them & that
you'll never understand.

So bearing this in mind, I'll
tell you that I hadn't slept
when the curtains allowed a
blue glow into the bedroom

& the street's resident
seagulls alerted each other to
something dropped & soaked
in brownish gutter-water.

In less time than it took for
me to grope my way to the
window & pull the curtains
open, the flock had scalped

the top crust from the loaf &
got their beaks into the pale,
soft cushion underneath. I
opened the window.

Show some respect, I wanted
to say. The drizzle continued
to swirl around the lampposts
& the lampposts

continued their competition
with the weak sunlight & the
gulls continued eating almost
as if no-one was watching.

Vanity with a Breakfast of Apples

The street runs from east
to west. On mornings like
this the terrace houses
frame a perfect view of
the mountains wearing
their coats of chartreuse
green. I had such plans:
plums with honey &
natural yogurt, Japanese
omelette-rolls, American-
style pancakes so thick
you could sleep inside
them. A good friend of
mine once said 'An apple
requires absolutely no
thought' & I think about
this in the corner shop
when I see a hundred
wonky copies of my own
face glazed onto the skins
of a hundred apples. No,
what I should say is, I'm
trying to think about this
but instead I'm thinking
about the moth that has
kept me turning late into
these last three nights – its
eyes when it singed its
feet on the bare lightbulb.

Bowls, Plates & Cups in a Garden with a Shower of Rain

Seen in this condition, like
gleaming menhirs against the
dripping trees, the crockery
seems so divorced from use

I could forget for a minute
that it was me who brought
them out to the garden, that I
had reasons,

that given the time of day
these reasons most likely
involved lunch, that lunch
likely involved soup:

a gazpacho in fact, partly on
account of the weather
forecast with its promise of
bubbling tarmac,

partly in the hope that among
the cubes of pepper, red
onion & cucumber I might
find a few more details

to piece into the story which
I know ends with me in an
all-night self-serve restaurant
in Madrid five years ago

pale & sweaty under the
fluorescent tube-lights — a
reason I had kept secret
even from myself until

this moment standing dumb
by the back door, in the
middle of a red mess from
the dropped tureen.

Nocturne with a Bottle of Sparkling Wine

Because I have no
answer to the question
of cava or prosecco,
I'm making a list of all
the things I remember:
that we were
sequestered in the front
downstairs bedroom,
that a few guests were
still in the kitchen, that
it happened between 3
and 5 in the morning,
that he would move out
of that house two days
later, that neither of us
had bought the wine,
that it really should
have been served
chilled but when we
passed it between us,
drinking straight from
the bottle, its slightly
fusty warmth made it
all the more delicious.

A Gift of a Melon

When you open it,
you won't really
have opened it: it
will still be wrapped
up in itself, in its
ridged & musty
skin. I think maybe
this is part of the
fun, one reason why
the   smoothest,
roundest   fruits
command   such
dizzying expense.

Yes, I'm beginning
to see why a melon
might just be the
perfect thing to
offer when the dead
are pressing their
hungry   mouths
against the paper-
thin divide which
keeps them out of
our   towns,   our
houses. I hope you
enjoy it.

Poem on the Perturbation of Cucumbers

There may come a
time when you'll
walk into your
kitchen still half
asleep & see four
cucumbers laid
parallel on an
enamel plate &
placed on a section
of the countertop
which at this time of
day in this season
just happens to be
where the window
sets down its bright
rhombus & you'll
think to yourself *this
is a perfect example*
& for the rest of the
day the question of
what? will follow
you to the bus, to
work, will sit with
you as you eat lunch,
making you spill
your coffee, &
things will only get
worse when you
realise the closest
you can get to

knowing how it feels
is to say it's almost
like when you know
that you have
dreamed but can't
remember the
situation of your
dream, the details,
which is much like
walking around
wearing trousers
taken down from the
line just slightly too
soon.

Aubade with Quince Paste & Stilton

How might I account for
this amplitude of pink?
As I understand it, a
quince's rind is yellow,
its   innards,   when
exposed, are yellow-
white. It is three days
after my twenty-second
birthday & I'm sitting at
the   kitchen   table,
spreading quince-paste
over   wheat   germ
crackers & trying to
work out some reason,
some logic for this
cerise. The cheese, I
comprehend. The cheese
is blue because during
the maturation process
its crust was pierced &
the   entry   points
colonised by mould &
yes! it accents the paste
beautifully, but this, I
suspect,   is   just
coincidental & doesn't
answer anything, really.

I go back to bed &
dream about walking
through a hailstorm of
miraculous medals.

The Curve

after Juan Sánchez Cotán's 'Still Life with Quince, Cabbage, Melon and Cucumber'

As clouds monopolise
a beautiful sky, so most
of the frame is filled
with nothing. The only
point of contact is
where a leaf sprouting
from the quince's stem
involves itself with a
length of string which
ends in a bouquet of
cabbage-leaves. The
quince is understudy to
the sun; its light is
reflected in the juicy
surface of the melon,
its stippled heart of
seeds. The yellow of
the quince's bruised &
burnished rind is
imitated in the tip of
the cucumber which
cantilevers out from
the concrete shelf &
almost begs for you to
take it in your hand.

ACKNOWLEDGEMENTS

'10 Game Fowls' was originally published in *Ambit*. 'Aubade with Half a Lemon' was originally published in *The Curfew Tower is Many Things*. I would like to acknowledge The Society of Authors for an Eric Gregory Award in 2015, & the financial freedom this afforded me to write this pamphlet.

I would like to thank Manuela & Stephen, for their editorial help & for The Lifeboat; Sinéad Morrissey, for reading the first drafts first & for her years of teaching; the staff & students & past-students of the Seamus Heaney Centre; Eamon & Tara & Caitlin, for the last three houses; Mary, for coffee & books & talk; my family, for being.